HAYNES EXPLAINS
CHRISTMAS

Owners' Workshop Manual

Published in September 2017

A catalogue record for this book is available from the British Library

ISBN 978 1 78521 152 2

Haynes Publishing, Sparkford,
Yeovil, Somerset BA22 7JJ, UK
Tel: +44 (0) 1963 440635
Website: www.haynes.com

Haynes North America, Inc.,
861 Lawrence Drive, Newbury Park,
California 91320, USA

Printed and bound in Malaysia

Cover image from Getty Images

Illustrations taken from the
Haynes Midget and Sprite
Owners Workshop Manual

Written by **Boris Starling**
Edited by **Louise McIntyre**
Designed by **Richard Parsons**

Safety first!

Christmas is a dangerous time. Alcohol is flammable, for a start, either literally (be careful when lighting the brandy) or metaphorically (family members having a few sherbets too many and then it all kicks off). Having an actual tree in the house is every bit as dumb an idea as it sounds when written down. Luckily new workforce regulations require Santa Claus to have a foreman in a hi-vis jacket present at all times. This foreman is of elvish descent and is called Elfan Safety.

Working facilities

Designated Christmas cook will be working in a kitchen which would just about be big enough if everyone would kindly push off and leave me alone. Designated TV channel changer requires full and exclusive use of a three-seater sofa. Designated dog walker has all the space in the world as everyone too full to accompany them. Designated Santa Claus still trying to work out how to get his 56in tummy down a 50in chimney and back up again.

Contents

Introduction

There are a few immutable truths to life. Every year, policemen look younger, politicians get more useless, and Christmas starts earlier. There's even a term for this: 'Christmas creep' (not to be confused with the pervy one from Accounts who tries it on with you, and in fact with anyone and everyone, at the office party – see 'dealership social activities').

Gone are the days when the Christmas run-up meant 1 December onwards, as though retail was nothing but a giant Advent calendar. Nowadays, no arbitrary mark is too early. Black Friday (in itself a ghastly American import)? Halloween? The clocks going back? Christmas has become a hybrid of Pac-Man and Godzilla, marching back across the months and chomping everything in its path.

Let Christmas begin on August Bank Holiday. No: let it begin the day England are knocked out of the World Cup or the Euros by a footballing titan like Andorra or Bhutan. May Bank Holiday? Easter? Valentine's Day? New Year? And suddenly you're back at 25 December and Christmas has literally eaten itself. Which is appropriate, given the gluttonous nature of the event.

Roy Wood famously wished it could be Christmas every day. Well Roy, old son, you've got your wish.

About this manual

The aim of this manual is to help you get the best value from Christmas. It can do this in several ways. It can help you (a) decide what work must be done (b) tackle this work yourself, though you may choose to have much of it performed by external contractors such as your wife, who is almost certainly 1,000,000% more organised than you could ever dream of being, or that nice Mr Bezos from Amazon whose remorseless algorithms make his company almost – but not quite – as efficient as your wife.

The manual has drawings and descriptions to show the function and layout of the various components. Tasks are described in a logical order so that even a novice can do the work. This is an awful lot more than you'll get in your average Christmas present, which will almost certainly be missing (a) the show-you-how (b) a vital part (c) any necessary batteries (d) all three.

⚠ Dimensions, weights and capacities

Overall height

Christmas tree ....

6.7in too tall for the room because someone thinks he's too good for the tape measure

Beer cans consumed ....

When placed one on top of the other: 238,890 miles. Just a few more tinnies and you could have reached the moon. Lightweight.

Overall weight

Average man ....

Average woman ....

1 December: 80kg; 31 December: 110kg

1 December: 50kg; 31 December: 50kg

That's what happens when you do all the cooking and everyone else does all the eating.

Consumption

Quality Street ....

12 tins per household per week.

Except the strawberry and orange ones. No-one likes those. What do you mean, you do? Really?

Mince pies ....

Brussels sprouts ....

1 per minute during daylight hours.

0. Seriously. I gave them to the dog.

Can't you smell?

Engine

Stroke ....

very probably, given all the eating and drinking.

Power ....

1500kW, mainly because next door's Christmas lights can be seen from space.

Torque ....

Bore ....

638Nm, to get the top off the cranberry sauce.

Alan from number 64 who always comes round for drinks on Christmas Eve and wouldn't leave until the 27th if he had the choice.

Redline ....

on carpet, while walking with the 45th glass of Chianti.

Purchasing

The purchase process varies considerably depending on the purchaser's gender. The man plans, budgets and spends ages getting everything right. The woman does none of this. Yeah, right.

Good Santa

You show your children the NORAD tracker online, which 'follows' Santa as he speeds round the world and keeps a running count of the presents he's given out. If weather and alignment are right, you take them out just after sunset to show them the space station zooming overhead and tell them it's Santa's sleigh.

Bad Santa

Santa's been down at the shopping centre for 12 hours straight. Santa asks the nice girl who offers him a cup of tea whether she could add a little whisky to it, you know, for flavouring. Santa says it's only what the folks at home leave out by their fireplaces, isn't it? Santa has one cup of 'tea' too many. Santa staggers around the shopping centre. Santa faceplants. Santa argues with security. Santa is caught on CCTV. Santa goes viral.

Scientists have calculated that Santa would have to travel at a speed of 6.7 million miles per hour on a sleigh weighing 2.3 million tonnes in order to deliver all the presents.

'YES, DARLING, A JERRYCAN AND JUMP LEADS ARE JUST WHAT I WANTED.'

FIG 5•1 **WHEN YOU CAN'T THINK OF ANYTHING TO BUY YOUR MUM**

⚠ A woman's guide to presents

Who you have to buy for:
- *Partner*
- *Children*
- *Parents*
- *Partner's parents*
- *Siblings, nieces, nephews, cousins, godchildren*
- *Partner's siblings, nieces, nephews, cousins, godchildren*
- *Yourself (direct result of partner's uselessness)*

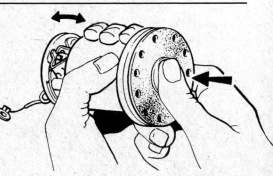

FIG. 5•2 **HOME-MADE PRESENT FOR THE MAN IN YOUR LIFE**

Schedule and planning:

1) No later than the summer solstice on 21 June, draw up spreadsheet listing all necessary recipients, maximum spend per person, suitable presents based on interests/age, and cross-referenced to previous years to avoid duplication.

2) Get especially exercised by what to buy partner as (a) anything he likes he will just have bought himself already (b) anything you give him he will assume to be a Trojan horse in your plan to remake him as you want.

3) Go online to price comparison and other retail websites, factoring in upcoming sales, currency movements, seasonal crazes and sundry additional relevant factors.

4) Adopt the kind of ruthless organisation which would shame the military. Colour-code purchases on receipt and stack them neatly in an area of the house subject to two-step verification password control and lockdown.

5) Maintain delineation of presents by using different wrapping paper per distinct set of recipients.

6) For those recipients who won't be seen over festive period, post in good time to beat Christmas rush. For those who will be seen but necessitate travelling, store neatly in car boot. For those who will be seen on Christmas Day itself, stack neatly beneath tree.

7) Indignantly refute all accusations of being anal.

⚠ A man's guide to presents

Who you have to buy for:

- *Partner. (If single, no-one, which is a total bonus.)*

Schedule and planning:

1) Maintain usual schedule (five-a-side, curry, Friday nights on the pop).

2) Become vaguely aware that Christmas is approaching due to increased frequency of parties.

3) Wait till Christmas Eve.

4) Not the morning of Christmas Eve, either. The afternoon. Late afternoon.

5) Panic.

6) Run to shops. Stop halfway to get breath back as all that partying has left you a little short of peak physical condition.

7) Look round frantically with head swivelling like Linda Blair's in *The Exorcist*, and maybe making about as much sense too (also possibility of pea-green projectile vomiting depending on length of run in previous point).

8) Remember four precious words. 'Shit in a basket'. Not an injunction, but a description. A selection of body wash, lotion, soap etc. in a basket. Women love that stuff.

8) Only realise once you're home that you bought her that last year too.

9) Don't worry. She won't remember. Will she?

1-LITRE BOTTLE OF WHITE LIGHTNING

PRESSURISED DELIVERY SYSTEM

FIG 5•3 **WHEN YOU SHOULD BE OUT BUYING PRESENTS. BUT YOU'RE NOT.**

⚠ What a present says

Present	What you think it says	What she thinks it says
Electronic fitness monitor	'We can exercise together.'	'You're fat.'
Bathroom scales	'You can check the results of that exercise.'	'You're fat.'
A diet book	'New Year, new you.'	'You're fat.'
Gift card	'You'll choose what you want better than I will.'	'I can't even be bothered to think of a present.'
Vacuum cleaner	'You're houseproud.'	'You're a domestic servant.'
Lingerie (Santa-themed)	'You can look sexy and festive at the same time.'	'Lingerie = good. Santa costume = OK. Combination = v poor.'
Unusual jewellery	'It would really suit you because you're a bit quirky.'	'You're having an affair, you bought this for her but you gave it to me by mistake.'
Puppy	'You're so good with animals, and anyway just look at him. He's so cute.'	'Guess who'll be feeding it, walking it, taking it to the vets and everything else.'
Power drill	'You're a strong independent woman who's beyond being confined by gender roles.'	'Oh, you've opted out of DIY as well as everything else now, have you?'
Mini-fridge	'For you to store all those amazing puddings you make.'	'For you to store all the lager it seems you can't live without.'
Sex toy	'We can spice things up in the bedroom.'	'You're outsourcing your marital duties to a piece of plastic. Nice one. Thanks.'
Nothing	'We have everything already. We don't need to give each other presents.'	'Bye!'

From the dealership

Round-robin letter

A family you don't see from one year to the next sends pages of A4 detailing their myriad accomplishments in a tone of pitch-perfect humblebragging. Get one of these, and you've been smugged. Goes something like this:

'Wow! We can hardly believe where the last 12 months have gone! So much has happened, and we've barely been at home – Courchevel, Antigua, Dubai, Umbria and South Africa, and that was just the first half of the year. John was

lucky enough to make partner this year, which means he's working even harder than before (hard to believe that's possible!) but of course the pay rise is some compensation. Jane has been project managing the renovation of our holiday home in the Dordogne (there goes the money from John's pay rise, and probably more besides!) Archie got A* or A in all 44 of his GCSEs, and Bella is in the county hockey team.

Dealing with the letter:

i) Mark it as though it were an essay, highlighting factual inconsistencies and poor grammar, and send it back to the sender.

ii) Email them asking why the son-in-law, whose achievements were so lauded in years 2007–16 inclusive, has now been airbrushed from history in a frankly Stalinist manner following his divorce from Perfect Eldest Daughter.

iii) Send one yourself to all your friends with a (hopefully) fictional account of your own annus horribilis, written in the requisite absurdly jocular tone. 'Christopher is earning excellent money selling drugs in the local park, though he has decided to take a five-year sabbatical in the Wormwood Scrubs area of west London.'

INSERT 'TRUTH' AT 1. RETRIEVE 'BOASTFUL FAKERY' FROM 2

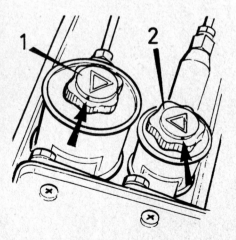

FIG 5•4 **ROUND-ROBIN PRINTING PRESS**

⚠ Letter euphemisms

What they say...	What they mean...
James is always away on business	James is having an affair
Susie is enjoying her tennis lessons	Susie is having an affair too
We had an amazing silver wedding party	You weren't invited
And are already looking forward to our golden one in 25 years' time	You won't be invited to that one either
Hannah has taken to motherhood like a duck to water	A more appropriate aquatic simile would be 'Hannah is drinking like a fish'
We had an amazing holiday. So nice to spend time with each other	We'll be paying off the credit card till 2040 and we sat in resentful silence most evenings
Matilda has a seriously fun group of friends	If one or more of them doesn't end up in a Young Offenders' Institution, I'll eat my hat
Henry's exam results were very good	He scraped a pass in all his subjects. God knows how. Must have been that private tutor we spent a fortune on
We've enjoyed debating the politics of the day with friends and family	We've had furious arguments about Brexit and no longer speak to half the people we know
Susie is finding herself increasingly involved with charity work and was on the committee for the local ball	Susie has to find something to do when her tennis coach isn't available
The dogs are still on good form but beginning to slow down	Rare and precious is the morning when I manage to get them outside before they've fouled the carpet
Our garden is looking lovely	Our garden is looking better than next door's
Hope you and yours are well	We have no idea what your family's names are
We must must MUST catch up this year	We will never see each other again

Fuel

If Christmas is about one thing above all (yes yes, apart from peace on earth and goodwill to all men and all that boo-ya), it's about food. And drink. That's two things. Oh. But anyway. Christmas is a time for eating your own bodyweight, washing it down with enough booze to have felled Oliver Reed, and then repeating three times a day. But it's not always plain sailing on HMS Yuletide.

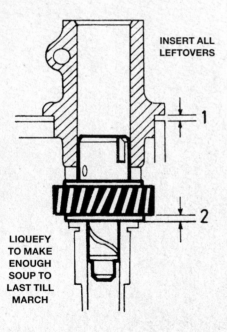

INSERT ALL LEFTOVERS

1

2

LIQUEFY TO MAKE ENOUGH SOUP TO LAST TILL MARCH

FIG 5•5 **THE GREAT BOXING DAY BLENDER**

a) Brussels sprouts. Why? Seriously? Does anyone actually like them? If they're that great, why don't they get wheeled out the other 364 days of the year?

b) 'Mince pies' not 'minced pies'. Grammar pedants (every Christmas home needs one) will point this out to you. Repeatedly.

c) It's important to use wine when cooking. Some of it may even go into the food rather than the chef.

d) Yes, of course you can still eat the turkey if you drop it on the floor. Have you seen how much the damn things cost?

e) Bad news: easy to confuse the brandy butter base with the bread sauce. Good news: brandied bread sauce isn't bad.

f) If you stock up on Christmas booze in November it will all get drunk long before Christmas. Trust me on this.

g) Run out of milk? Use Bailey's. Tea, coffee and cornflakes all taste better that way.

⚠ Perpetual motion

A Go to pub having put turkey in the oven.

Remember you still have Christmas pudding. Apply flaming brandy. Flames quickly spread to tablecloth. Grab fire extinguisher. Soak pudding and guests.

Return from pub to find oven door has been left slightly open. Turkey only half-cooked, oven knobs melted.

Turn up heat to cook turkey quicker.

Check on turkey's progress. Still semi-raw. Turn up heat still further.

Find that potatoes and parsnips are burnt to such a crisp that they set off the smoke alarm.

Be crushed underfoot by elderly relatives stampeding like wildebeest as alarm plays havoc with their hearing aids.

B Clamber on table to turn off the alarm.

Take turkey out of oven. Prepare to carve.

FIG 5•6

Find that in smoke alarm stampede earlier someone knocked the ham to the floor without anyone noticing. Except the dog. Who is now being sick.

Take turkey out after further hour. Find it dry as a bone. Get blamed by mother-in-law anyway. Go to Plan B: back-up ham.

Mother-in-law insists turkey needs another hour. Oblige her for the sake of peace and quiet.

Environment

Ah, the tree. What is it with people? There are folks living in a tiny attic flat who insist on buying a tree bigger than the one Norway plonks in Trafalgar Square every year, and then there are folks living in barn conversions with double-height ceilings who buy a tree roughly the size of a bonsai to make sure it fits. To all y'all, here are two words: tape, measure.

Once you've got the size more or less sorted, your next choice is this:

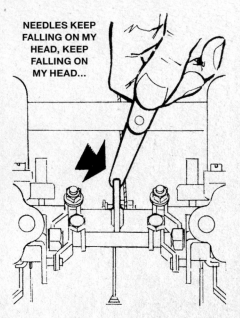

NEEDLES KEEP FALLING ON MY HEAD, KEEP FALLING ON MY HEAD...

FIG 5•7 **ADJUSTING THE TREE BASE**

Artificial or real?

Whichever you choose, at some stage you'll wish you'd gone the other way. If you go artificial you'll find yourself hankering after that natural pine smell. If you go real you'll find yourself hankering after something whose needles don't poke you in the eye every time you come within five feet of it.

Choosing a tree isn't the half of it

Working out the pros and cons of various types of tree – Norway spruce or Nordmann fir? Blue spruce or Fraser fir? Serbian spruce or Douglas fir? **FOR GOD'S SAKE JUST GIVE ME THAT ONE OVER THERE YES THAT ONE THANK YOU** – isn't even the half of it either. (That's two halves and you still haven't got to the point – Ed.)

Getting it upright, straight and stable, that's the problem. Oh, any fool can do two out of three.

i) Upright and stable – but leaning over gracefully like the Leaning Tower of Pisa.

ii) Straight and stable – but straight flat on the floor doesn't count.

iii) Upright and straight – but only for a few seconds till it crashes down onto the TV.

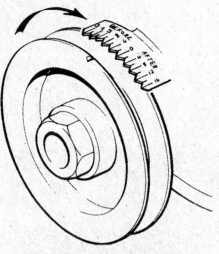

FIG 5•8 **CUTTING THE TREE DOWN TO SIZE. BEFORE: A GIANT REDWOOD. AFTER: A STICK**

Getting all three at once requires the kind of engineering chops usually found in the guys who build skyscrapers. Even when you have finally managed it, and remembered to put water in the base so it doesn't die round about 22 December, it still may come crashing down. If so, carefully question three categories of suspect:

1) Children
2) Old people
3) Pets

If all three have alibis, then the fault is with you, the tree-putter-upper. No, it did not 'just fall over', not unless you live in an earthquake zone.

Decorations

Don't be surprised to find that when you bring the decorations out of storage they're all packed away higgledy-piggledy and it takes you ages to find what you're looking for. That's because you put them away at the end of last Christmas when you were tired, emotional and toxic. In particular, fairy lights may be hideously tangled. The good news is that you will untangle them as long as you remain patient. The bad news is that the untangling process may take you until Boxing Day, by which time you'll have missed the whole thing.

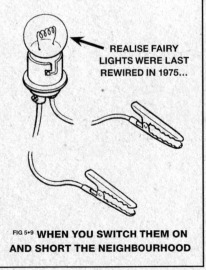

REALISE FAIRY LIGHTS WERE LAST REWIRED IN 1975...

FIG 5•9 **WHEN YOU SWITCH THEM ON AND SHORT THE NEIGHBOURHOOD**

Headlights and sidelights

When it comes to lighting up your house at Christmas, there are three schools of thought.

School of thought 1
(not to be confused with School Of Rock, School's Out or Me And Julio Down By The School Yard)
Holds that Christmas lights should be kept inside the house only: on the tree, maybe tastefully wrapped round the banister too, that kind of thing.

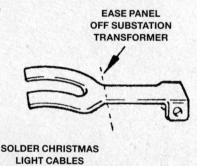

EASE PANEL
OFF SUBSTATION
TRANSFORMER

SOLDER CHRISTMAS
LIGHT CABLES
TOGETHER

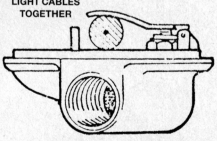

FIG 5•10 **LIGHTING YOUR HOUSE 101: HACKING THE NATIONAL GRID**

School of thought 2
Allows for some external lighting as long as it's understated and used sparingly. Over the front door is OK. Maybe some lanterns at ground level on the way from front gate to door. Lights must be white only and may not flash.

School of thought 3
Is the Anything Goes school. These guys' houses make the Blackpool Illuminations look like North Korea at night. You name it, they've got it, all lit to within an inch of its life by tens of thousands of coloured bulbs. Santas, reindeers, candy canes, three wise men, penguins – where did they come from? – snowmen, snowwomen, snowchildren, snowdogs, Christmas trees, Christmas messages (polite ones, not ones inviting Santa to do something biologically impossible) and so on.

You can see these houses from space. Up on the International Space Station, there are astronauts saying 'there's London…. There's Paris…. And there's the Smiths at number 52, look, they've really gone for it this year, haven't they?'

Nothing brings out the snobbery and class divide (without which Britain would simply stop functioning, let's face it) quicker than houses like this. Which side of the divide are you on?

⚠ The great divide

Pro	Con
It's just a bit of fun.	If that's your idea of fun then I'm never going on holiday with you. It's vulgar and gaudy, that's what it is.
It brightens the place up, and God knows we all need that during those long winters.	A nuclear strike from Moscow would also brighten the place up, but that doesn't mean we should welcome it.
People come from miles away to have a look at it.	Exactly! People do come from miles away. As far as I'm concerned that's where they should bloody well stay.
It raises lots of money for charity.	It costs more than that in electricity.
The kids love it.	The kids love Transformer movies too. The kids are not good arbiters of taste.
Christmas is the time for tasteless tat.	Tasteless tat is tasteless tat no matter what time of year it is.
It gets me into the festive spirit.	Spirits get me into the festive spirit.
It means the council will upgrade our street's electricity supply.	I still can't run more than two appliances at once.
All that light scares burglars away.	The flashing blue lights in your front garden always make me think the police have just arrived.
It's only for a month a year.	So's hay fever.

Finally, no extravagantly illuminated house is complete without having neighbours who leave their own house in darkness apart from an arrow pointing to the mini-Vegas and the word 'GIT'.

Family cars

The first line of Leo Tolstoy's *Anna Karenina* is, famously, 'all happy families are alike; each unhappy family is unhappy in its own way.' Except, he might have added, at Christmas, where even the least dysfunctional and most stable families can find themselves a wrapping paper's thickness away from Armageddon. Booze, tensions, crappy weather and houses crammed with people: what could possibly go wrong?

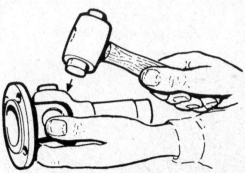

FIG 5•11 **BASH REPEATEDLY OVER OWN HEAD BY 4 P.M. ON CHRISTMAS DAY**

1) The first rule of Christmas Club: just survive it. Aim no higher than that. Enjoyment is a bonus. Survival is paramount.

2) The second rule of Christmas Club: see first rule.

WARNING

On the twelfth day of Christmas teenagers gave to me: 12 unchanged loo rolls, 11 lightbulbs left on, 10 greasy saucepans, 9 hours of wifi, 8 sweaty sports kits, 7 piles of washing, 6 'not fair' protests, 5 slammed doors, 4 requests for cash, 3 lost phones, 2 unmade beds and complaints about the lack of TV.

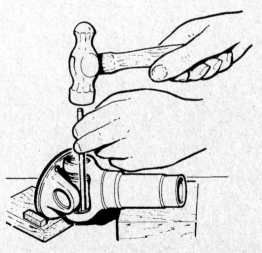

FIG 5•12 **TOOLS FOR KEEPING YOURSELF SANE AT YULETIDE**

You want some more?

Who do you think I am? Santa Claus? OK, OK. Here goes.

3) If possible, make people come to you rather than vice versa. Christmas travel is a nightmare whichever way you cut it: there's a reason Santa takes the aerial route during the anti-noise-pollution no-fly-zone times. Motorways are packed day and night as everyone's had the same 'let's beat the rush' idea you have: train services are up the swanny, down the wazoo and round the bend due to some genius' idea to start Engineering Works on 21 December.

4) Every family has one weird relative. If you don't know who it is, look in the mirror.

5) Mental, bonkers, bananas, nuts, barmy: you name it, kids will go it. Sugar, presents, games, excitement can all get too much. Get them out of the house if possible (for a walk in the afternoon, that is, not locked out all night, tempting though it may be) to let off some steam. And also try to see Christmas through their eyes and remember what it was like for you as a child. Does it really matter if house rules about tidiness and bedtime get broken for a day or two?

6) It doesn't matter how old you are or how high-powered your job is: when you and your siblings reassemble under your childhood roof, you will instantly revert to your childhood roles. Two FTSE 100 chief executives can easily end up wrestling over the TV remote control and shouting 'Mum! Muuuuuuuum! Make him give it back!'

7) Even the most difficult guest is just that – a guest. And soon they will be gone. Unless it gets really bad (as in really really bad, as in DEFCON 1 bad), just grin and bear it. You can't change who they are, but you can control how you react to them. Has your mother-in-law given you cold cream for ageing skin? Thank her profusely and put it in the drawer for presents to recycle on to someone else. Probably back to her next Christmas, the mean old witch.

When a great-aunt you haven't seen for 20 years says 'my, how you've grown!' the correct response is NOT 'my, how you've aged!'

In-car entertainment

Think of Christmas on TV and chances are you'll think of the Queen's Speech. Now, you may reckon she says pretty much the same thing year each time, perhaps even exactly the same thing. 'Sorry chaps, ran out of time to write something, here's the transcript from 1961, let's just go with that, no-one will notice.'

But spare a thought for her too. Every year, every single year, she's just about to sit down for her turkey, a couple of glasses to the good, when she has to drop everything and go and talk to 10 million total strangers, many of them semi-comatose. You'd think they'd just record it in advance and spare her the trouble, wouldn't you?

Even in this digital age, one analogue Christmas tradition remains sacrosanct: buying the bumper Radio Times edition and going through it page-by-page circling in red all the programmes you want to watch.

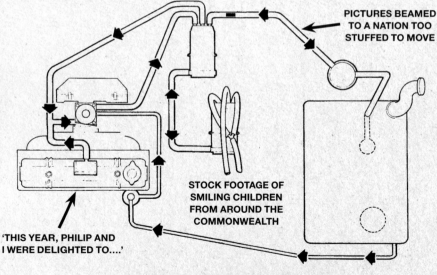

PICTURES BEAMED TO A NATION TOO STUFFED TO MOVE

STOCK FOOTAGE OF SMILING CHILDREN FROM AROUND THE COMMONWEALTH

'THIS YEAR, PHILIP AND I WERE DELIGHTED TO....'

FIG 5•13 **THE QUEEN'S SPEECH: A SCHEMATIC**

⚠ Christmas TV

Christmas specials of popular TV shows

Usually filmed in August and therefore a triumph of the thespian art to pull off the tinsel-and-party-hat look when it's 30 degrees outside and all the crew off-camera are in shorts and T-shirts.

'Event' TV dramas

Run over two or three nights between Christmas and New Year. Most recently, adaptations of Agatha Christie novels such as *And Then There Were None*. People forced into a house together, tension, murderous intent, wild accusations and mutual suspicion – it's a perfect reflection of Christmas, let's face it.

Christmas films

A flying snowman in *The Snowman*. A flying car in *Chitty Chitty Bang Bang*. Lots of cars and Michael Caine in *The Italian Job*. Not many cars but lots of Michael Caine and quite a few British soldiers in *Zulu*. Quite a few British soldiers in *Escape To Victory*, and quite a few Nazis too. A German bloke (but not a Nazi) played by a British bloke in *Die Hard*, and some businessmen too. And a nasty businessman in *It's A Wonderful Life*, as Christmassy a film as *The Snowman* itself.

The marquee Christmas advert

These always follow the same rules. Friendship with animals or snowmen? Check. Slowed-down, stripped-back faux-indie version of famous song covered by the chanteuse du jour? Check. Subtle but unmistakeable advertising for supermarket chain almost certainly hammering their own suppliers' margins down to as near zero as possible and that's not very Christmassy is it? Check. More snow than the Antarctic even though it's set in the Home Counties which sees a white Christmas on average about once every two and a half centuries? Check. Emails from your friends linking to the advert and saying 'OMG THIS IS AMAZING, YOU'LL CRY!' Check.

50% EXPERTLY MANUFACTURED EMOTION

50% EXPERTLY PRESENTED SALESMANSHIP

FIG 5•14 **DISSECTING THE CHRISTMAS ADVERT**

Sound system

During the Cold War, the CIA would use Christmas music as part of their resistance-to-interrogation training. If an agent could listen to *I Believe In Father Christmas* and *Rockin' Around The Christmas Tree* on an endless loop for 48 hours, they figured, a stint of KGB torture would seem like a walk in the park by comparison. 'Yuri, we will never break this Americanski. Listen to him. He says he will deck the halls with boughs of holly.'

There are some Christmas songs which are good. But there are many more which are bad, and some of those are very, very bad.

⚠ Top three Christmas songs

Fairytale Of New York
The Pogues and Kirsty MacColl
Drunken and sentimental, full of anger and resentment but also hope and love, it's the perfect Christmas song. Shane McGowan and Kirsty McColl spark off each other so well, and if you don't shed a tear during the soaring chorus about the boys of the NYPD choir singing 'Galway Bay' check your pulse, as you may already have gone to the great Christmas tree in the sky.

Christmas In Hollis
Run DMC
Hip-hop Christmas songs are a niche genre, so to say this is the best in that category may be faint praise. That doesn't matter, however, as it's a great Christmas song regardless of genre. And it has a classic video too, featuring a mischievous elf who messes up all Santa's plans so that the members of Run DMC don't get their desired black bucket hats to add to their already extensive collection.

Merry Xmas Everybody
Slade
The song which reputedly still makes Noddy Holder £500,000 a year. But having heard Amy McDonald sing it acapella, you realise it's actually a love song – to families, to love, to nostalgia, to peace and goodwill if only for a day. Good on yer, Noddy, even if we do still need to talk about your spelling. Cum On Feel The Noize? Skweeze Me Pleeze Me? Spellcheck is your friend here, my man.

Special mention:

Benny Hill's *Ernie, The Fastest Milkman In The West, Mr Blobby* by, er, Mr Blobby and *Can We Fix It?* by Bob The Builder have all been Christmas Number Ones.

PRESSING THE PERFECT CHRISTMAS SINGLE

A

FIG 5•15 **OH, WHO ARE WE KIDDING? IT'S ALL DIGITAL DOWNLOADS NOW**

⚠ Bottom three Christmas songs

Millennium Prayer
Cliff Richard

Just about beats out Mistletoe and Wine *and* Saviour's Day *from the* CCC (Cliff's Christmas Collection). Were it not for the self-imposed 'only one Cliff track' rule, the lad could have been looking at a clean sweep here. But it's Christmas, so let's spread the podium places around a bit. Anyway,* Millennium Prayer. *Basically saying the Lord's Prayer over a pretty basic backing synthesizer track.*

Do They Know It's Christmas?
Band Aid

Sure, it was for a good cause, and sure, they wrote it in a hurry. But (a) Sting singing about the 'bitter sting of tears' was cringeworthy at the time and gets even more so in retrospect (b) Bono yelling 'tonight thank God it's them instead of you' isn't exactly the spirit of Christmas, is it? (c) Christianity is the single largest religion in Ethiopia so yes, they probably do know it's Christmas.

Wonderful Christmastime
Paul McCartney

Obviously took over Cliff's barely used synth from Millennium Prayer *for an equally anodyne backing track. For six years McCartney was a major part of the greatest band in history. And then this. The anti-Beatles. Even Wings ('only the band the Beatles could have been', according to Alan Partridge) might have thought twice about recording this one.*

Recreational vehicle

Christmas games are fun for all the family…. until everyone takes it all a little too seriously and it all ends in tears. As it always does.

There are quite a few considerations to be taken into account when playing Christmas games. First, that these games can expose and widen decades-old psychological faultlines which would have had Freud himself purring. Second, that the contestants have already spent more time with each other over the previous few days than they have over the rest of the year combined. Finally, all that food and booze has made them VERY punchy. The optimum time limit for any Christmas games is therefore:

$$O = (S \times T) - 10,$$

Where O is optimum time,
S is stimulant (alcohol for the adults, sugar for the children),
T is tantrum, and 10 is minutes.

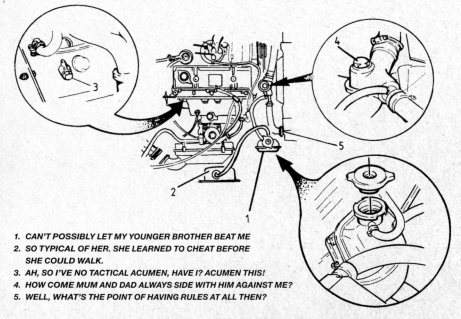

1. *CAN'T POSSIBLY LET MY YOUNGER BROTHER BEAT ME*
2. *SO TYPICAL OF HER. SHE LEARNED TO CHEAT BEFORE SHE COULD WALK.*
3. *AH, SO I'VE NO TACTICAL ACUMEN, HAVE I? ACUMEN THIS!*
4. *HOW COME MUM AND DAD ALWAYS SIDE WITH HIM AGAINST ME?*
5. *WELL, WHAT'S THE POINT OF HAVING RULES AT ALL THEN?*

FIG 5•16 **EMOTIONAL JENGA – UNPACKING THE PSYCHOLOGY OF CHRISTMAS GAMES**

⚠ Christmas games

1. Charades

Best played a little drunk, as charades is no fun when it's too easy to guess but great fun when the actor can't act out properly and the guessers can't guess. Also lets you know which of your family are secretly more competitive than you thought and end up brooding for half an hour afterwards that they just can't believe that nobody got *Prisoner of Azkaban* and really how stupid are you all?

2. Scrabble

Best not played drunk as it's hard enough sober. Throws up lots of possible words which sound almost as though they're real but turn out not to be. Finglet, for example, is not a singlet for fingers, no matter how hard you try to convince the assembled company that it is. Also, be the 'no-you-get-a-double-letter-score-but-not-a-triple-word-score' stickler for rules. There's always one in Scrabble and it might as well be you.

3. Monopoly

This one causes more arguments than anything else in human history, including religion, politics and the correct pronunciation of the word 'controversy'. Literally anything in Monopoly can cause a fight.

i) I want to be the car. No, I want to be the car.
ii) Why do you stack your money in one big pile? You should divide it into different denominations and tuck them under the edge of the board. No you shouldn't, because it makes the board tilt and then everything slides off their squares.
iii) Utilities. No one ever wants them. Stations, too.
iv) Hey, Mr Banker, are you sure you're keeping your money and the bank's money separate?
v) Yes, I know this is the fifth round in a row I've landed on Mayfair which you own, but there's no need to rub your hands together quite so gleefully.

Don't even think about playing Risk. The twin prospects of world domination and shifting alliances mean it ends in tears even quicker than other board games.

Dealership events

The office Christmas party. Did those four words just make you shudder? They did, didn't they? And with good reason.

You spend eight hours a day five days a week with these people, and the only thing you have in common with most of them is that you tread the same piece of carpet. Why in the name of Beelzebub's balls would you choose to spend even a minute more in their company than you have to? It's bad enough having to deal with your family at Christmas, let alone your workmates. Where did I put that 'HERMIT WANTED' advert?

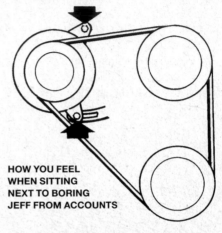

HOW YOU FEEL
WHEN SITTING
NEXT TO BORING
JEFF FROM ACCOUNTS

FIG 5•17 **THE ENDLESS TREADMILL OF EXISTENCE**

In fairness, there are several positive aspects to the office party:

1) An afternoon out of the office

....

2) The chance to make a small fortune by running a book on who'll be first on the dancefloor and then cleaning up when the chairman, a 100-1 rank outsider whom literally no-one had backed, is first to strut his stuff before leading the entire finance department in an enthusiastic rendition of *Oops Upside Your Head*.

....

3) Er… that's it.

WARNING

The best way to think of an office party is to imagine that a police officer is reading you your rights. You have the right to remain silent, and should probably do so – especially when it comes to telling your boss exactly where he can shove his job. If you don't, you will find that anything you say is used against you in a disciplinary hearing, and that you may well need a senior colleague during questioning.

In contrast, there are many more areas for potential or actual disaster:

1) Secret Santa. Buy a £5 present for someone you hardly know. Chances of this present being in any way desirable or desired = zero. Time you'll spend worrying about what to buy = 100 hours.

2) Overly cheery emails with too many exclamation marks!!!!! AND CAPITAL LETTERS which can't disguise the essential, nay existential, futility of holding a once-a-year party in either the pub you visit every week or indeed the office building you visit every day.

3) Alcohol and loose tongues. Someone will always (a) confess undying love for a colleague (b) engage the boss in a free and frank exchange of views (c) spill secrets they shouldn't know to people who shouldn't hear. None of these are in any way good.

4) Despite the fact that everyone's menu choices have been made a month in advance and checked, double-checked, triple-checked and no-returns-confirmed in the interim, there will always be a mix-up on the starters and a whole heap of grief about dietary requirements.

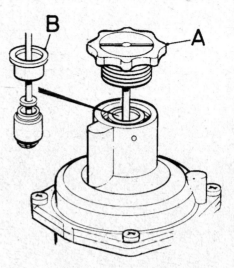

FIG 5•18 **TESTING YOUR ALCOHOL STREAM FOR BLOOD LEVELS**

5) No matter how much drink has been taken and whatever the provocation, sexual or otherwise, remove no clothes other than jacket, keep hands resolutely unballed into fists at all times, and never ever be the last one to leave, as if you are you'll be stuck with the Christmas creep.

Some companies like to have their Christmas parties in January. This is very possibly the only idea worse than having a Christmas party in December.

Viral advertising

Like every other aspect of life nowadays, Christmas does not exist unless it's recorded on several social media platforms at once for your friends to 'like' when they should be spending time with their families but they're not because the reason they're online to 'like' your stuff in the first place is that they too are recording every beat of their own Christmases for you to 'like'.

FILTERING OUT ALL BUT THE VERY BEST IMAGES

FIG 5•19 **PRESSURE ON: HOW TO GAUGE OTHER PEOPLE'S CHRISTMAS**

Essential DOs and DON'Ts

✓ DO Wish everyone a Merry Christmas. Once.

✓ DO Put up a couple of photos which are sweet and good-natured without being too obviously superior.

✓ DO Use social media sparingly. It's Christmas. You survived plenty of them without a mobile phone, didn't you? Hell, your grandparents survived plenty without a phone of any sort, and getting bombed by the Luftwaffe to boot.

✗ DON'T Take pictures of your presents. How old are you? Six?

✗ DON'T Instagram your Christmas lunch. Everyone's having exactly the same as you. Just eat the damn food.

✗ DON'T Virtue signal. 'So far I've donated to a toy drive for disadvantaged kids, put an armful of selection boxes into a food bank collection point, I'm working my Christmas Eve off so a colleague can spend the day with her grandma and am volunteering at a soup kitchen on Christmas Day.'

⚠ Cold-weather protection

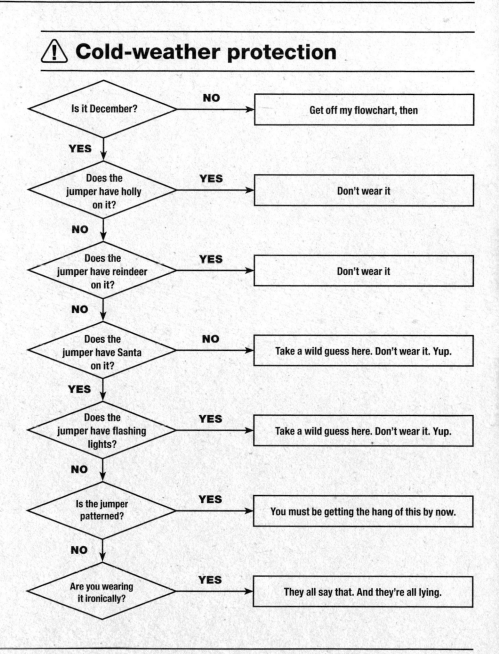

Is it December? — **NO** → Get off my flowchart, then

YES ↓

Does the jumper have holly on it? — **YES** → Don't wear it

NO ↓

Does the jumper have reindeer on it? — **YES** → Don't wear it

NO ↓

Does the jumper have Santa on it? — **NO** → Take a wild guess here. Don't wear it. Yup.

YES ↓

Does the jumper have flashing lights? — **YES** → Take a wild guess here. Don't wear it. Yup.

NO ↓

Is the jumper patterned? — **YES** → You must be getting the hang of this by now.

NO ↓

Are you wearing it ironically? — **YES** → They all say that. And they're all lying.

Year-end sales quota

New Year's Eve is like the death of a pet: you know it's going to happen, but somehow you're never really prepared for how truly awful it is. With the possible exceptions of first sexual encounters, the England football team at every major tournament and (some) James Bond films, nowhere is the gap between expectation and reality more pronounced than on New Year's Eve.

Every year you get revved up and think, yeah, this is going to be a great night, we're going to go crazy – and every year you end up covered in your own vomit (if it's a barely acceptable evening) or a total stranger's (if it's not).

Solution

Luckily we're on hand to tell you how to get out of this hideousness. It's not as though being slumped half-cut on the sofa watching *Jools Holland's Hootenanny* is an unmitigated barrel of laughs, let's face it, but at least the interlude between venue and bed is a flight of stairs rather than four hours on rain-lashed streets waiting for an Uber that never arrives.

What you need here is (a) a ready-made list of excuses (b) the fallback that these excuses are actually true. It's just that you've left some part of them unsaid. Let *Haynes Explains* explain.

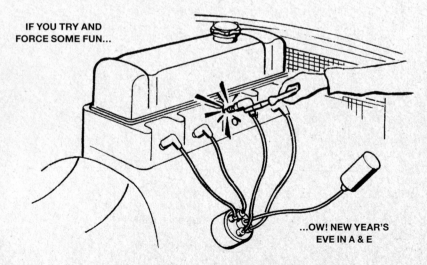

IF YOU TRY AND FORCE SOME FUN...

...OW! NEW YEAR'S EVE IN A & E

FIG 5•20 **NEW YEAR'S EVE PATENT ENJOYMENT GENERATOR**

⚠ New Year's Eve excuses

The bit you say	The bit you leave out
You go on. I'm still getting changed …	… into my pyjamas. At 6 p.m.
I have to go to my sister's. She's sick …	… of me using her as a way to get out of things.
I've already arranged to hook up with friends …	… called Ross, Rachel, Phoebe, Chandler, Joey and Monica. On boxset.
The Uber driver hasn't arrived yet …	… because I never called him.
Really? I never read your message …	… because it said 'NYE' in the title and so I deleted it without opening.
My dogs really hate fireworks …	… but they're with my Mum in the country.
The babysitter can't make it …	… because we told her we didn't need her.
Mark had a really bad New Year's Eve experience …	… 25 years ago. Which he hasn't thought about for 24 years.
Yes, of course I like your friends …	… to stay as far away from me as possible.
You could come round to mine …	… tomorrow.
Ever since lunchtime I've been drinking …	… tea
I just looked at the map and the party is such a long way away …	… from New Zealand. But it's only 10 minutes from here.
I can't do crowds because I get flashbacks to 'Nam …	… Cheltenham, that is.
I'd rather wait for Chinese New Year …	… and stay in and watch telly then too.

New model year

It's always good to make a list of New Year's resolutions. You did it last year, and the year before, and the year before that. Since they've all been barely used (which is why your fat/thin bank account/body ratio remains so badly out of whack), just dust them off and use them again this year.

The UN Security Council has made more than 2,350 resolutions in its history. Not one of those resolutions has been to go to the gym more often.

Getting started

It's important to get off on the right foot with New Year's resolutions. Let's say you're going to eat more healthily. That's good. But there's probably a lot of junk food still in the house, right? Thought so. And you don't want to let that go to waste. So eat all that junk food up before you go all quinoa.

As for exercise, well, there's surely a niche for someone to develop a mixed-use commercial property area which is a gym for the month of January and a pub for the other 11 months of the year. They do say 'give the customers what they want', don't they?

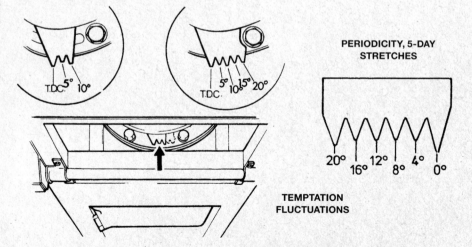

FIG 5•21 **RESOLUTIONOMETER: MEASURING YOUR STRENGTH OF WILL**

⚠ Dry January

Normally the words 'dry' and 'alcohol' appear together only on the sherry bottle. If you do decide to stop drinking for a month, for heaven's sake don't announce it publicly or, worse, ask for sponsorship. Since when did not doing something become an achievement? No one sponsors you for not running a marathon, do they?

Do it for yourself

Quiet and stoic, like a frock-coated Victorian gentleman convinced that temperance is good for the character. You'll find you sleep better, which means you feel more alert in the mornings, which means you need fewer cups of coffee. Begone, twin curses of alcohol and caffeine! Maybe you're becoming a Mormon. Check you still have only the one wife, who may not even have noticed your new-found abstention on the grounds that anything clear in your glass is presumably vodka and tonic.

But January is an absurd month to give up the booze. You lose weight, but no one can see it under thick winter clothes. Better skin? Hard to tell when your face gets lashed by gale-force winds and driving rain the moment you step outside. And good luck dealing with the January credit card bills without a beer to hand.

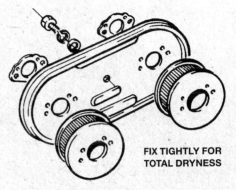

FIX TIGHTLY FOR TOTAL DRYNESS

FIG 5·22 **VACUUM-SEALING YOUR BOTTLES**

Sod it...

Start drinking again. It's not like you're an alcoholic. An alcoholic is someone you don't like who drinks as much as you do. So next time someone asks 'dry?', reply 'why?'

Basically, the only resolution you should make is not to make resolutions, and certainly to stop hanging out with people who either make them themselves or ask you what yours are.

⚠ Fault diagnosis

Fault	Diagnosis	Treatment
Cannot move due to gluttony.	It's Christmas.	Eat and drink some more.
Are in a dingy pub wearing a party hat with work colleagues.	It's Christmas.	Eat and drink some more.
Are about to kill family members	It's Christmas.	Eat and drink some more.
Are about to kill carol singers	It's Christmas.	Eat and drink some more.
Have spent 4.5 hours failing to put up tree.	It's Christmas.	Eat and drink some more.
No coconut Quality Street left	It's Christmas.	Eat and drink some more.
Think that an *Eastenders* Christmas looks positively peaceful in comparison	It's Christmas.	Eat and drink some more.
World War III about to break out over control of the remote control	It's Christmas.	Eat and drink some more.
Can't get 'Merry Xmas Everybody' earworm out of head	It's Christmas.	Eat and drink some more.
Have no peace on earth and feeling goodwill to no men	It's Christmas.	Eat and drink some more.

Conclusion

Christmas is a trying time for many people. But it's also an important one: a chance to pause and rest (even if sometimes it doesn't feel much like a rest) and step off the endless hamster wheel of work and modern life for even a few days. Imagine how long winter would feel without Christmas to break it up (unless you're one of those people who jets off to Barbados in the depths of winter, in which case you know what you can do and where you can do it, and yes, 64 pictures on Instagram of sunset behind a champagne glass is quite enough, thank you).

The bloke who taught me to drive longer ago than I care to admit would regale me (in between three-point turns and emergency stops) with his theory as to why Jesus couldn't have been born on 25 December. I can't remember the exact details, because, you know, mirror-signal-manoeuvre and all that, but I think the general gist was (a) star positions in the sky (b) weather (too cold for the shepherds to be out). In between his day job, this bloke had fixed 16 September as the most likely actual Christmas Day. Not sure it's going to catch on any time soon, Mike. Sorry.

And no matter how much we grumble about Christmas, there are always plenty of people who would love to be in a house full of people and noise with an enormous plate of turkey but for one reason and another aren't. To paraphrase Oscar Wilde, the only thing worse than spending Christmas with your family is not spending Christmas with your family. If this book came in your stocking or from under the tree, I hope your Christmas has been better than some of the examples in here, and that you have a New Year full of happiness which lasts and resolutions which don't.

Titles in the Haynes Explains series

Now that Haynes has explained Christmas, you can progress to our full size manuals on car maintenance (to ensure the in-laws get home quickly), *Running Manual* (to remove that festive spare tyre), *Home Extension Manual* (for peace and goodwill next year) and *Astronaut Manual* (extreme tinsel avoidance).

There are Haynes manuals on just about everything – but let us know if we've missed one.

Haynes.com